D0618276

Delicious
smoothies

Delicious

smoothies

Love Food ® is an imprint of Parragon Books Ltd

Parragon
Queen Street House
4 Queen Street
Bath BA1 1HE, UK

Copyright © Parragon Books Ltd 2008

Love Food ® and the accompanying heart device is a trademark of Parragon Books Ltd

All rights reserved. No part of this publication may be reproduced, stored in a retrieval system or transmitted, in any form or by any means, electronic, mechanical, photocopying, recording or otherwise, without the prior permission of the copyright holder.

Photography by Günter Beer
Home economy by Stevan Paul

ISBN 978-1-4075-3308-7

Printed in China

Notes for the reader
• This book uses imperial, metric, and US cup measurements. Follow the same units of measurement throughout; do not mix imperial and metric.
• All spoon measurements are level: teaspoons are assumed to be 5 ml, and tablespoons are assumed to be 15 ml.
• Unless otherwise stated, milk is assumed to be lowfat and eggs are medium. The times given are an approximate guide only.
• Some recipes contain nuts. If you are allergic to nuts you should avoid using them and any products containing nuts.
• Recipes using raw or very lightly cooked eggs should be avoided by infants, the elderly, pregnant women, convalescents, and anyone suffering from illness.

Contents

Introduction

Just because we know what is good for us doesn't mean that we always do what is right. For example, we all know that nutritionists recommend five portions of fruit and vegetables a day and most people recognize that it is important to start the day with breakfast. However, life is lived in the fast lane these days and it is difficult to fit in shopping and cooking with the demands of work and family life.

Smoothies can make a considerable contribution to resolving this dilemma. They can be made in minutes, so saving precious time in the kitchen. They are full of nutrients and count towards the recommended 'five a day'. Many are positive powerhouses and provide a real energy boost first thing in the morning or at any time when you feel that you are running out of steam. This book is a great place to start your smoothie love affair, and the 40 fabulous recipes for

stunning smoothies will get your taste buds tingling!

Most of the equipment required for making smoothies will already exist in any reasonably well-stocked kitchen. No specialist expensive tools are required, although you might like to choose some that speed things up or make life a little easier. Blenders, food processors, or liquidizers will make smoothies in seconds, so it is well worth investing in one of these if they are not part of your kitchen already. A range of cook's knives will cut through the preparation in no time, and a separate chopping board kept exclusively for fruit and vegetable preparation is essential.

The benefits of making smoothies a part of your life are endless. They contain no artificial flavors, colors, or preservatives, some of which are known to have adverse effects on people with allergies and on children. By preparing your own smoothies, you know exactly what

ingredients have been used, so there are no unpleasant surprises or hidden quantities of saturated fats or sugar. They offer a tasty and interesting alternative to commercial products, cost less, are usually healthier, and can be adapted to your personal taste. The natural sweetness of fruit means that fruit smoothies are an easy way to reduce sugar intake without compromising taste. And when you have a few pieces of fruit left in your fruit bowl at the end of the week, why not use them up in a smoothie—providing they are still in good condition? With so many delicious combinations to choose from, there will always be something different for you to try.

The recipes in this book have been chosen because the ingredients complement each other perfectly, creating mouthwatering, delicious smoothies. Turn to the chapter entitled 'Berry Brighteners' when raspberries and strawberries among others are in season. Kids in particular will adore the Banana & Strawberry Smoothie, a classic that will never go out of fashion. When you are feeling more adventurous, turn to 'Totally Tropical'—and try the Papaya Sweet & Sour Smoothie for something very special. 'Fresh Flavors' looks to orchard fruits such as apples and plums for inspiration, resulting in cool creations such as Perfect Plum Shake. 'Cool & Creamy' is for those indulgent days when only creamy, smooth concoctions will do. The Coffee Banana Cooler is sure to become a firm favorite! But there is no reason why you can't experiment with your own ideas—you are limited only by your imagination. Try experimenting with vegetables and create a nutrition-packed vegetable smoothie—a great way to get those essential vegetable nutrients into kids or teenagers. Take advantage of the seasonal fruit and vegetables on offer, and make smoothies part of your diet all year round.

Bursting with flavor, crammed with goodness, made in minutes, and inexpensive—it is no wonder that smoothies are so fashionable.

Berry Brighteners

serves 2

1¹/₂ cups blueberries

²/₃ cup cranberry juice

²/₃ cup plain yogurt

berry smoothie

Put the blueberries and cranberry juice into a blender and process for 1–2 minutes, until smooth.

Add the yogurt and blend briefly to combine. Taste and add honey, if you like. Blend briefly again until thoroughly combined.

Pour into chilled glasses and serve.

serves 2

1/3 cup raspberries

1/2 cup strawberries, hulled

1 cup plain yogurt

1 cup milk

1 tsp almond extract
(optional)

2–3 tbsp honey, to taste

raspberry & strawberry smoothie

Press the raspberries through a nylon strainer into a bowl using the back of a spoon. Discard the seeds in the strainer.

Put the raspberry purée, strawberries, yogurt, milk, and almond extract, if using, into a blender and blend until smooth and combined.

Pour the smoothie into chilled glasses, stir in honey to taste, and serve.

serves 2

scant 1/2 cup strained plain yogurt

scant 1/2 cup water

scant 1 cup frozen blueberries, plus extra to decorate

blueberry thrill

Put the yogurt, water, and blueberries into a blender and blend until smooth.

Pour into glasses and top with whole blueberries.

serves 2

2/3 cup frozen black currants

4 scoops of black currant sherbet

scant 1/2 cup sour cream

2 tbsp black currant cordial

1 tbsp water

sugar, to taste

mint leaves and whole blackberries, to decorate

black currant bracer

Put the black currants, sherbet, sour cream, cordial, and water into a blender and blend until smooth. Taste and sweeten with a little sugar if necessary.

Pour into glasses. Drizzle over some cordial, decorate with the mint leaves and blackberries, and serve.

serves 2

1 banana, sliced

1/2 cup fresh strawberries, hulled

heaping 2/3 cup lowfat plain yogurt

banana & strawberry smoothie

Put the banana, strawberries, and yogurt into a blender and blend for a few seconds until smooth.

Pour into glasses and serve immediately.

serves 2

4 tbsp orange juice

1 tbsp lime juice

scant 1/2 cup sparkling water

2 1/3 cups frozen summer
fruits (such as blueberries,
raspberries, blackberries,
and strawberries)

4 ice cubes

summer fruit slush

Pour the orange juice, lime juice, and sparkling water into a
blender and blend gently until combined.

Add the summer fruits and ice cubes and blend until a slushy
consistency has been reached.

Pour the mixture into glasses and serve.

serves 2

generous 3/4 cup blackberries

scant 1 cup blueberries

scant 1/2 cup ice-cold water

2/3 cup plain yogurt

black & blue

Put the blackberries, blueberries, water, and yogurt into a blender and blend until smooth.

Pour into glasses and serve.

serves 4
3 cups cranberries, thawed
if frozen

scant 2 cups cranberry juice,
chilled

1¼ cups plain yogurt

2–3 tbsp honey

cool cranberries

Place the cranberries and juice in a blender and blend until smooth. Add the yogurt and 2 tablespoons of the honey and process again until combined. Taste and add the remaining honey if necessary.

Pour into chilled glasses and serve.

serves 2

2 large ripe peaches

generous 2/3 cup red currants

3/4 cup ice-cold water

1–2 tbsp clear honey

peach & red currant sunset

Halve the peaches and discard the pits. Coarsely chop the peaches and put into a blender.

Keep 2 stems of red currants whole for decoration and strip the remainder off their stems into the blender. Add the water and honey and blend until smooth.

Pour into glasses and decorate with the remaining red currant sprigs.

serves 2

1/2 cup frozen raspberries

1 1/4 cups sparkling mineral water

2 scoops black currant sherbet

raspberry & black currant slush

Put the raspberries and water into a blender and blend until smooth.

Add the sherbet and blend briefly until combined with the raspberry mixture.

Pour into glasses and serve.

Totally Tropical

serves 4

handful of cracked ice

2 bananas

1 cup pineapple juice, chilled

1/2 cup lime juice

slices of pineapple,
to decorate

perky pineapple

Put the cracked ice into a blender. Peel the bananas and slice directly into the blender. Add the pineapple juice and lime juice and blend until smooth.

Pour into chilled glasses, decorate with slices of pineapple, and serve.

serves 2

2 ripe bananas

3/4 cup lowfat plain yogurt

1/2 cup skim milk

1/2 tsp vanilla extract

honey, for drizzling

banana breakfast shake

Put the bananas, yogurt, milk, and vanilla extract into a blender and blend until smooth.

Pour into glasses, drizzle with honey, and serve.

serves 2

1 ripe papaya, peeled, seeded, and chopped

1/2 fresh pineapple, peeled and chopped, plus extra to decorate

2/3 cup soy milk

11/4 cups soy yogurt

tropical smoothie

Place all the ingredients in a blender and blend until smooth.

Pour into glasses, decorate with chopped pineapple, and serve.

serves 2

9 oz/250 g ripe soft papaya

3/4 cup ice-cold water

juice of 1 lime

slices of papaya, to decorate

papaya sweet & sour smoothie

Peel the papaya, discarding any seeds. Cut into chunks.

Put the papaya chunks into a blender with the water and lime juice and blend until smooth.

Pour into glasses and decorate with slices of papaya.

serves 3

scant 1 cup whole blanched
almonds

2¹/₂ cups dairy-free milk

2 ripe bananas, halved

1 tsp natural vanilla extract

ground cinnamon,
to decorate

almond & banana smoothie

Put the almonds into a blender and blend until very finely chopped. Add the milk, bananas, and vanilla extract and blend until smooth and creamy.

Pour into glasses and sprinkle with cinnamon to decorate.

serves 2

1 cup plain yogurt

3¹/₂ oz/100 g galia melon, cut into chunks

3¹/₂ oz/100 g cantaloupe melon, cut into chunks

3¹/₂ oz/100 g watermelon, cut into chunks

6 ice cubes, crushed

wedges of melon, to decorate

melon refresher

Pour the yogurt into a blender. Add the galia melon chunks and blend until smooth.

Add the cantaloupe and watermelon chunks along with the ice cubes and process until smooth.

Pour the mixture into glasses and decorate with wedges of melon. Serve immediately.

serves 2

1 wedge of watermelon,
weighing about 12 oz/350 g

ice cubes

slices of watermelon,
to decorate

watermelon refresher

Cut the rind off the watermelon. Chop the watermelon into
chunks, discarding any seeds.

Put the watermelon chunks into a blender and blend until
smooth.

Place ice cubes in the glasses. Pour the watermelon mixture over
ice and serve decorated with slices of watermelon.

serves 2

14 oz/400 g canned guavas,
drained

1 cup ice-cold milk

guava goodness

Place the guavas in a blender and pour in the milk. Blend until well combined.

Strain into glasses to remove the hard seeds. Serve.

serves 2

scant 1/2 cup pineapple juice

4 tbsp orange juice

41/2 oz/125 g galia melon, cut into chunks

5 oz/140 g frozen pineapple chunks

4 ice cubes

slices of orange, to decorate

melon & pineapple crush

Pour the pineapple juice and orange juice into a blender and blend gently until combined.

Add the melon, pineapple chunks, and ice cubes, and process until a slushy consistency has been reached.

Pour the mixture into glasses and decorate with slices of orange. Serve immediately.

serves 4

1 watermelon, halved

6 tbsp fresh ruby grapefruit juice

6 tbsp fresh orange juice

dash of lime juice

slices of watermelon, to decorate

watermelon sunset

Deseed the melon if you are unable to find a seedless one. Scoop the flesh into a blender and add the grapefruit juice, orange juice and lime juice.

Blend until smooth, pour into chilled glasses, decorate with slices of watermelon, and serve.

Fresh Flavors

serves 2

2 ripe apples, peeled and
coarsely chopped

2 oz/55 g strawberries, hulled

juice of 4 oranges

sugar, to taste

slices of apple,
to decorate

apple cooler

Put the apples, strawberries, and orange juice into a blender and blend until smooth.

Taste and sweeten with sugar if necessary.

Decorate with slices of apple and serve immediately.

serves 2

1 ripe pear, peeled and cut into quarters

1 apple, peeled and cut into quarters

2 large red plums, halved and pitted

4 ripe dark plums, halved and pitted

generous 3/4 cup water

slices of apple or pear, to decorate

orchard fruit smoothie

Put the pear, apple, plums, and water into a small pan. Cover tightly, then set over medium heat and bring slowly to a boil. Take off the heat and let cool. Chill.

Put the fruit and cooking liquid into a blender and blend until smooth.

Pour into glasses, decorate with slices of apple or pear, and serve.

serves 2

2 large ripe Anjou pears

scant 1 cup frozen
raspberries, plus extra
to decorate

generous 3/4 cup ice-cold
water

honey, to taste

pear & raspberry delight

Peel the pears and cut into quarters, removing the cores.
Put into a blender with the raspberries and water and blend
until smooth.

Taste and sweeten with honey if the raspberries are a little
sharp.

Pour into glasses and decorate with raspberries. Serve.

serves 2

1 green tea with Eastern
spice tea bag

1 1/4 cups boiling water

1 tbsp sugar

2/3 cup ripe yellow plums,
halved and pitted

green tea & yellow plum smoothie

Put the tea bag in a teapot or pitcher and pour over the boiling water. Let infuse for 7 minutes. Remove and discard the tea bag. Let chill.

Pour the chilled tea into a blender. Add the sugar and plums and blend until smooth.

Serve immediately.

serves 2

9 oz/250 g ripe plums

generous ¾ cup water

1 tbsp golden granulated
sugar

4 scoops of frozen yogurt
(plain) or ice cream

slices plum and crumbled
biscotti, to decorate

perfect plum shake

Put the plums, water, and sugar into a small pan. Cover tightly
and simmer for about 15 minutes, or until the plums have split
and are very soft. Let cool.

Strain off the liquid into a blender and add the frozen yogurt.
Blend until smooth and frothy.

Pour into glasses and decorate the rims with slices of plum.
Sprinkle over the crumbled biscotti and serve.

serves 2

8 ice cubes, crushed

2 tbsp cherry syrup

generous 2 cups sparkling water

fresh whole cherries on swizzle sticks, to decorate

cherry kiss

Divide the crushed ice cubes between two tall glasses and pour over the cherry syrup.

Top off each glass with sparkling water. Decorate with cherries on swizzle sticks and serve.

serves 2

4 small firm pears

2 heads elderflowers, freshly picked (or a dash of elder-flower cordial)

1 strip lemon zest

1 tbsp brown sugar

4 tbsp water

generous ¾ cup lowfat milk

langues de chat biscuits, to serve

elderflower & pear smoothie

Peel the pears and cut into quarters, discarding the cores. Place in a pan with the elderflowers, lemon zest, sugar, and water. Cover tightly and simmer until the pears are very soft. Let cool.

Discard the elderflowers and lemon zest. Put the pears, cooking liquid, and milk into a blender and blend until smooth.

Serve immediately with langues de chat biscuits.

serves 2

1 apple, peeled, cored, and diced

1 cup chopped celery

1¼ cups milk

pinch of sugar (optional)

salt (optional)

strips of celery, to decorate

apple & celery revitalizer

Put the apple, celery, and milk in a blender and blend until thoroughly combined.

Stir in a pinch of sugar and some salt if you like.

Pour into chilled glasses, decorate with strips of celery, and serve.

serves 2

9 oz/250 g jar morello
cherries

2/3 cup strained plain yogurt

sugar, to taste

whole fresh cherries,
to decorate

cherry sour

Put the cherries with their liquid into a blender with the yogurt,
then blend until smooth.

Taste and sweeten with sugar if necessary.

Pour into glasses, decorate with cherries, and serve.

serves 2

4 medium ripe plums, pitted

generous 3/4 cup ice-cold milk

2 scoops luxury vanilla ice cream

plum fluff

Put the plums, milk, and ice cream into a blender and blend until smooth and frothy.

Pour into glasses and serve immediately.

Cool & Creamy

serves 2

4 cups strawberries, hulled

1/2 cup coconut cream

2 1/2 cups pineapple
juice, chilled

strawberry colada

Halve the strawberries and place in the blender.

Add the coconut cream and pineapple juice and process until smooth, then
pour into chilled glasses and serve.

serves 2

$^2/_3$ cup milk

2 tbsp chocolate syrup

14 oz/400 g chocolate ice cream

grated chocolate, to decorate

chocolate milkshake

Pour the milk and chocolate syrup into a blender and blend gently until combined.

Add the chocolate ice cream and blend until smooth. Pour the mixture into tall glasses and scatter the grated chocolate over the tops.

Serve immediately.

serves 2

1¹/4 cups milk

¹/2 tsp allspice, plus extra
to decorate

5¹/2 oz/150 g banana ice
cream

2 bananas, sliced and frozen

spiced banana milkshake

Pour the milk into a food processor and add the allspice. Add half of the banana ice cream and blend gently until combined, then add the remaining ice cream and blend.

When the mixture is well combined, add the bananas and process until smooth.

Pour the mixture into glasses, add a pinch of mixed spice to decorate, and serve.

serves 2

1 cup milk

scant 1/2 cup coconut milk

5 1/2 oz/150 g vanilla ice cream

2 bananas, sliced and frozen

scant 1 1/2 cups canned pineapple chunks, drained

1 papaya, deseeded and diced

grated coconut, to decorate

tropical storm

Pour the milk and coconut milk into a blender and blend gently until combined. Add half of the ice cream and blend gently, then add the remaining ice cream and blend until smooth.

Add the bananas and process well, then add the pineapple chunks and papaya and blend until smooth.

Pour the mixture into tall glasses, scatter the grated coconut over the tops, and serve.

serves 2

1 cup frozen strawberries

scant $1/2$ cup light cream

generous $3/4$ cup cold whole milk

1 tbsp superfine sugar

mint leaves, to decorate

strawberries & cream milkshake

Put the strawberries, cream, milk, and superfine sugar into a blender and blend until smooth.

Pour into glasses and serve decorated with mint leaves.

serves 2

scant ¹/₂ cup milk

¹/₂ cup peach yogurt

scant ¹/₂ cup orange juice

1 cup canned peach slices,
drained

6 ice cubes, crushed

strips of orange zest,
to decorate

peach & orange milkshake

Pour the milk, yogurt, and orange juice into a blender and blend gently until combined.

Add the peach slices and ice cubes and blend until smooth. Pour the mixture into glasses and decorate with strips of orange zest.

serves 2

1¹/₄ cups milk

4 tbsp instant coffee powder

5¹/₂ oz/150 g vanilla ice cream

2 bananas, sliced and frozen

coffee banana cooler

Pour the milk into a blender, then add the coffee powder and blend gently until combined. Add half of the ice cream and blend gently, then add the remaining ice cream and blend until well combined.

When the mixture is thoroughly blended, add the bananas and blend until smooth.

Pour the mixture into glasses and serve.

serves 2

3/4 cup black cherries

3 large scoops luxury white
chocolate ice cream

2/3 cup milk

black & white smoothie

Halve and pit the cherries. Put them into a blender and blend
until smooth.

Add the ice cream and milk and process briefly to mix well.

Pour into glasses and serve.

serves 2

1¹/2 cups pineapple juice

¹/3 cup coconut milk

5¹/2 oz/150 g vanilla ice cream

1 cup frozen pineapple chunks

grated fresh coconut, to decorate

2 scooped-out coconut shells, to serve (optional)

coconut cream

Pour the pineapple juice and coconut milk into a blender. Add the ice cream and blend until smooth.

Add the pineapple chunks and process until smooth.

Pour the mixture into scooped-out coconut shells or tall glasses and decorate with grated fresh coconut. Serve.

serves 2

generous 3/4 cup milk

scant 1/4 cup light cream

1 tbsp brown sugar

2 tbsp unsweetened cocoa

1 tbsp coffee syrup or instant coffee powder

6 ice cubes

whipped cream and grated chocolate, to decorate

mocha cream

Put the milk, cream, and sugar into a blender and process gently until combined.

Add the unsweetened cocoa and coffee syrup and process well, then add the ice cubes and blend until smooth.

Pour the mixture into glasses. Top with whipped cream, then scatter over the grated chocolate and serve.